This Journal Belong to :

_____

Date

Date

Date

Date

Date

Date

Date

Date

Date

Date

Date

Date

Date

Date

Date

Date

Date

Date

Date

Date

Date

Date

Date

Date

Date

Date

Date

Date

Date

Date

Date

Date

Date

Date

Date

Date

Date

Date

Date

Date

Date

Date

Date

Date

Date

Date

Date

Date

Date

Date

Date

Date

Date

Date

Date

Date

Date

Date

Date

Date

Date

Date

Date

Date

Date

Date

Date

Date

Date

Date

Date

Date

Date

Date

Date

End of my Journal

Made in the USA
Monee, IL
16 December 2022

22244721R00057